Subjects Suitable
for Poetry

Charlotte Lit Press
Charlotte Center for Literary Arts, Inc.
PO Box 18607
Charlotte, NC 28218
charlottelit.org/press

Cover design by Micaelah Scott Peterson of The Farthest Pixel
Author photo by Ed Cheney

ISBN: 978-1-960558-00-8

PROUD MEMBER

[clmp]

COMMUNITY OF LITERARY MAGAZINES & PRESSES
W W W . C L M P . O R G

Subjects Suitable for Poetry

Gary Phillips

Charlotte Center for Literary Arts, Inc.
Charlotte, North Carolina
charlottelit.org

Contents

As the Land Changes So Shall We Follow Bright and Kind

I went to visit my mother by the sea,
finding her there talking with the rooks and gulls,
pale body shimmering with a bold delight.

I went with my children to the near mountains,
riding in the back seat like a child myself,
crags, living streams, ancient woods, fog and mayhem.

Walking to town from my farm in the country
took me days; I slept in fields and woodlands,
watching the country change, nature emerging

as if from a long and dangerous travail,
awake alive and green, as a gray fox
crossed the stream and sat, listening.

Singing a blessing to all I have married,
I went along bold, capricious and weary,
following the fox following the bright song.

Weather Bound

You need to understand I grew up at the knife-edge end of
subsistence culture / North Carolina, 1960s, strung between the
Cherokee foothills and Pisgah.

My father prayed for white bread and sturdy shoes when he was
a child / a boy who sometimes walked barefoot 14 hours a day
behind a mule's ass.

We followed old ways of foraging, employed beagle hounds, gigs,
tackle and shotgun. Between chores and pleasures the outside was
inside our thin house; I love weather

in all its forms, from sheeting rain come down the holler in a wave
to a blanket of snow. I greet the weather like a companion, speak
to it in tones

and prayers, bond my spiritual and emotional life to it, hard rain,
desert sere / thunder and lightning above rough seas, bitter cold
under a quilt of stars

I gave away my guns when I was in my twenties and joined
the peace movement. Turned away from that hardscrabble but
satisfying life, like a perfect academic wife

inside and tamed, hired and named, currying favors and closing
my windows at night / til ten years on and in full flight I landed
in Wales, on a 600-acre sheep farm by the sea

and on a rainy day that distilled me, with borrowed wellies and a hat.
I was set out with some companions, then the keeper placed
into my hands

a nineteenth-century Spanish double-barrel with silver inlay that
felt so right / I looked about to see where I was / the rain drilling
down

into the soft earth and saying rise, rise again, and a bird burst from the
wood / and up my arms went to the sky and the stock against
my shoulder fit; I shot

and the bird plummeted, while my heart beat the staccato of a
waterfall / and the rain fell and fell, where all dispersed but me and
gun and gamesmen.

I stayed the day and helped to put the birds away, hung on
tenterhooks to cure / for next week's meal. I was made to drink
a dram and dry my coat and eat a meal.

Then I went out again, to greet the rain.

Leonora

Leonora was a beekeeper maven and a bold, accomplished folklorist who studied women's fabrics, especially handmade quilts and all the domestic stories they told, making many friends of old women outside the world's ken, and holding vast riches of character.

Leonora must have asked some of the many who admired him, *who can I trust with this?* And several gave him my name as I can be trusted and lead with my heart, even in matters of business, especially in those matters.

Leonora used a variety of pronouns to describe themselves and I tried to follow, but they gave me an *old-man-pass* and never burdened me, though their friends who were many still argue about what they demanded to be called.

We talked for hours on the phone but never met, their soft West Virginia cadences familiar to my mountain past, both accents shouldered aside for access to a greater world, both deepening into twilight as we talked about our pasts, about their health, their dilemma, future, the house, the family in West Virginia who still treated them with a deep and troubling affection. They talked with their mother almost every day.

Leonora and I continued our conversation until the end: who to deliver the nineteenth-century spinning wheel to, the disposition of the house and tools, how to conduct a clothing giveaway for all his lovers and friends. For he had good style and closets full of leather, cotton, wool, and silk, mostly vintage and well-chosen, clean and pressed like applicants to a deep-South debutante affair but more punk. Definitely more punk.

On a Sunday afternoon I made a simple dinner for myself while we recited everything we treasured, which was much. We ended the conversation with declarations of affection and gratitude in rich hillbilly accents only our mothers would recognize. Leonora died the next day. The obituary was slight and inadequate, with only one pronoun.

Ruby and Darling

Ruby, I'm not your daddy. You shouldn't introduce me like that.

Darling, you're the closest thing to family I got. Would you rather I said sugar daddy?

Ruby, I'm not even close to being your sugar daddy. You pay the rent and almost all the bills around here. I'm just kind of a hanger-on with benefits.

Benefits? Every time your Social Security check come in we get dressed up and go out to dinner on it, don't we? So I have some benefits too. And nobody in my life ever gave me an all-over hot bath like you. It makes me wiggly just to think about it.

Wiggly? Is that some way to talk to an old man? And keep your hands on that steering wheel! You know it pleasures me to make your bath, to see all of you relaxing in that big tub and under my hands. Ruby, sometimes I can't believe what a sweet life I fell into in my old age, after everything I've been through.

There, you said it. Was that so hard? I met you when I was 12 years old and you come to visit my real daddy, who wasn't worth a shit compared to you. You gave me a kind of attention that woke me up and made me think about who I am. Who cares about all the years in between? They told me you were getting out of jail and I borrowed my brother's Cadillac and drove two hours to the penitentiary at 6 a.m. in the morning, not my usual time to do anything. So I got you—here you are, sitting right here. But a little too far away. Scooch on over closer. I like to feel your heat.

Woman, you are a wonder. So what's on tonight? The Supper Club? I got just enough change in my pocket to buy us a good steak and two beers.

No, honey, I don't want to see anybody tonight but you. I brought all my spa tools home from work; we are going to give your aching feet exactly what they deserve. You don't know how much I'm looking forward to that.

And what am I going to do for you, Ruby?

[...]

Silly. You are going to choose the music while I set up, something with a talking saxophone please, and you are going to open up the biggest bottle of red wine we have in the house and you are going to make dinner for us like you do almost every night, maybe a hot gumbo filé to give us strength, and after all that you are going to let me cry a little while I work on your feet and tell you my stories. When we're through you can comfort me any way you feel like. Is that okay?

Sounds like a dream, baby. You want white rice or dirty?

Death and the Maiden

Julia Rodrigues tended the garden
as when the old man was alive,
which is to say tenderly, obsessively,
as if the old man was alive and well:
teasing the roots of the *Brugmansia*
he smuggled from Argentina,
mixing its soil carefully, collecting seeds
to grind for their tropane alkaloids
as when the old man was alive,
awaiting visions, preparing for
her journey to the spirit world,
opening herself to the soft
admonishment of the ancestors,
sifting through the artifacts of
the greenhouse, now
that the old man
was no longer alive.

Waiting for Seed

Outside the window cardinals mass in the yew and rivercane. A young sassafras is bent under the weight of passerines. I think a wren is building a nest in Olin's old jacket near the barn. Good use for it, with Olin gone. What a difference one life makes, after all. There is no birdseed. I ordered some but nobody's coming up here in this storm. And I have people to feed and settle.

Olin's family. They don't know I am a horse in a barn aflame, looking for a way out. I am ready to kick a wall in, to fight against the sky, scream as the wind streams like a mane over my long and beautiful body. In a dead run to anywhere, just not here right now, not this pitiful barn and little bit of pasture. I'm bigger than this. Everybody says so.

Still, it has sheltered me, and there are corners where I have chewed into the wood enough to place my affection. Tender leather here and the smell of animals. After things calm down I will go outside, which is where I live anyway. I'll borrow a little molasses grain from the stock and spread it out on the long table under the pine. What's next I don't know, but birds will come.

Directions to the Richey House on Lick Branch

Well, I know where you're talking about
but I don't rightly think you can get there from here
in your little car, too low a carriage I think,
but if you want to try, and others have,

go off the highway at Bee Log and
take the first dirt road after the French Broad River.
Now ride it all the way to the end:

Mind that little branch just after
the fourth or fifth curve, the bridge is out
and you have to cross it with some care
but that ain't the bad part.

When you get to the very end, about thirteen miles
of hard road, it looks like you're at a cliff,
which you are—take that little road down to
Lick Creek and you're close, real close.

This *is* the hard part. You have to take that creek
up to her house, which is a little more than a mile,
only way to get there I swear but the scenery is pretty,
laurel blooming all up and down the valley right now.

Now don't take the creek if the water is up
or you'll never get your car back.
Just ease up in that creek bed
real slow-like, careful careful.

If the car gets hung on a rock
somebody will eventually come along and pull you out—
her neighbors love her that much.
Oh, you'll know the place, nothing else like it.

[...]

I don't know if she'll sing for you or not
but at some point or another she will
tell you to get on back the way you come,
which you better, believe me—

the alternative is possum gravy and
sleeping triple in a single bed, which
you don't look up to pardon me.

Nearly Winter

Late fall, nearly winter
a green tree frog came to live with us,
hidden among the cactuses and tropicals
we saved from the first hard frost.
Handsome, dapper in his lime-green coat with bone piping,
hiding in our small winter jungle during the day
and hunting long-legged cellar spiders while we sleep.
This morning at dawn he showed himself to me
then pulled in his legs as if in prayer.
I offered him water in a clay bowl
and he took it, after I looked away.

Field Peas

Shelling southern field peas
What a porch meditation
Each tight leathery jacket
Only a fingernail can separate
This is a spiritual ritual for me
Necessary, nourishing, tending
I call in my bold grandmothers
Singing, tasting the atmosphere

Crowders-purple hulls-cowpeas-African peas

Singing, tasting the atmosphere
I call in my bold grandmothers
Necessary, nourishing, tending
This is a spiritual ritual for me
Only a fingernail can separate
Each tight leathery jacket
What a porch meditation
Shelling southern field peas

Coyote

At walk in the dry mesic woodlands
above the muddy bouldered Haw,
alone among forest giants I know
a deep snowbank where foxes den.
Aim for a circle of white oaks
ancient hickories, sourwoods dancing
toward the light, beeches in a circle
a row of eastern red cedar trees
aging imperceptibly but certainly
as I am most certainly aging,
an old man in old woods, bone food
and leaf litter soon enough. To be
alone amidst such love such calm regard,
a borderland of slow easy conversations, death
ambling toward me like Coyote, smiling.

My Grandmother

Knew the sacred nature of her place:
A scrap of mountain above Cane River, on Big Creek,
the Blue Ridge a bowl above the barns.
I remember holding a handful of her skirt to keep up,
hunting creasy on a February morning,
our breath like the smoke of campfires,
air uncurling in the tiny valley, snaking
its slow way up the hills
almost visible.
Much of my grandmother's life was like that, almost visible.
We walked together.
I was proud to be with her, knowing her importance.
She pointed out the sacred places
among the rocks and pathways, under stone and by water,
the trees of worth,
the shy creatures of air and earth and sky.
She let me see they
meant no harm,
had their own ways
and business to perform.
We sat at the top of things
before the biscuit bag was opened,
together, looking down at her valley,
my hand in her lap,
mist rising in tatters.

Midrash

Hath the Spirit of the land forgotten to be gracious? Hath she in anger shut up her tender mercies? Selah. (Psalm 77)

Selah – lift up

Selah – fortissimo

Selah – sing loudly now

Selah – crash of cymbals, blare of trumpet

Selah – pause

Selah – pause now because your song is about to reveal a secret

Selah – so be it

Praise be – *Selah*

Praise and exalt the goddess – *Selah*

Selah – rock

Selah – stop and listen

Selah – please somebody sing

Selah – oh, choir-master!

Selah – preserve the truth

Selah – be honest and righteous

Selah – (with a sigh:) forever

Selah – measure, take the measure, change the measure, measure once/ cut twice

Selah – God is change

Selah – always

Selah – always yours

Figs

My father died and
I went down to pick his figs,
thinking to make a simple jam sweet
enough to absorb grief.
Inside the humming tree—mid August
and hot enough to make snakes mad—

I held a dancing
communion with yellow jackets,
red wasps, midge flies,
bumblebees, hornets, cow-killers,
working around the tree with
nimble, trembling fingers.

Did you know the great Bodhi tree was a fig?
That fig milk dissolves warts?
That one can pray inside the circle
of a father's ancient anger
and not be stung?

My Tender Body

Understanding now that when my father beat me
it was meant to hold me near.
He was punishing his loneliness,
not my tender body.

It was meant to hold me near
(a rune against his loss and fear)
one anchor cast into a pitching world.

He was punishing his loneliness,
terrified as he hovered, of his life
as tenant farmer, mill-hand, father,

not my tender body.
My pain was never more than his,
we made our bargains later
and washed them with his tears.

Class Will Out

The rich white men of my hometown met to judge me.
I thought it was an interview, but it was a hazing.
The stakes were high. Being paid to go to college

or work every summer in a cotton mill. They asked
me what my father did and how I learned to read, how
I could possibly have gotten an adequate education

in my little elementary school at the other end of
the county, and how I intended to better myself if
I stole such an award from the state university.

This was 1971, and no women were allowed to apply.
Apparently, redneck crackers were discouraged too.
I didn't even know enough to be mad. I had read my

Camus and written publishable essays, volunteered
with my church and even played on the football team
though I hated almost every minute of it. I came

prepared to talk about politics, literature (my specialty),
my God who impelled me, my good loving family if
need be but I never expected the lens of class to be

thrust at me like fire to an anthill. Their final speech:
*We haven't fielded a Morehead for years. Here's the
deal: Get rid of that mountain accent. We mean it.*

*We don't want, can't stand for you to go to
Chapel Hill and embarrass us with that hick talk.*
I spent a whole summer imitating the broad vowels

of midwestern commentators and newsmen, trimming
my Appalachian dialect with a broadax, murdering for
such little gain my good ancient grandmother tongue.

Cotton-Mill Blues

My mother was a weaver in a Southern textile mill, working on production, who left that work when she was sexually assaulted by her supervisor.

She and my father met each other and abandoned all others. I was born four months after the wedding, which was held in some preacher's living room. There are pictures of them dressed in nice clothes, looking like a pair of wild animals captured in headlamps.

My father came from a sharecropping family and turned to the cotton mills so he could earn cash and buy a car. He began as a sweeper, became a doffer, and finally settled into loom fixing, which he worked at until all the mills were shut down.

Have you read your Rick Bragg? *The Best We Ever Had* is the story of my family, my community, my class, which Autocorrect suggests I replace with "classmates," so afraid this money-ordered world is of how people live and die without recompense, fodder for the ever-extractive upper classes, like trees butchered and taken from a forest, like the coral and diamonds circling your elegant neck, like all the dead fishes in the sea.

Gurley and Nell

My father was born in the Cherokee foothills along the border between the Carolinas in 1929. His family were sharecroppers, which is a hard way to make a living in this world.

"What did you do when you were a kid?" I asked him once when I was seven or eight.

Walked behind a mule all day, he said, *mostly.*

He met Nell when he was six and she was two, a cotton jenny mule his father bought at the trade lot in Forest City. She had long ears, small hooves, a doleful gray face. And a suspicious disposition.

Two years later my father was pulled out of the fifth grade to work on the farm full time, which meant as always working with mules.

Gurley and Nell grew up together. When he graduated from farmwork to the textile mill he left the farm but brought the mule with him, along with all her tools: hames and harness, drag chains, one-row cultivators, walking plows, "fertilize" distributor, seeder, moldboard and more. They worked together almost every day, making a garden, hauling logs, pulling the wagon we kept in the center of the barn like a prized car.

They were a sight, talking to each other like old sisters when they were plowing up and down the rows. People would pull off the road to take their picture.

We grew a *lot* of potatoes, enough to last us the whole year until the next crop. One of my father's favorite moments was when it was time to dig up those potatoes. We would all gather in the field with wooden boxes while my father hitched Nell up to the biggest moldboard plow we had, with a curved metal blade that he cleaned carefully after each use and sharpened with a rasp. He would set the plow with Nell in the exact right place at the beginning of a 75-foot row of potatoes and yell, "Dig in, now!" and the little mule would set in her hooves and pull with all her might, while the moldboard tossed potatoes two or three feet up in the air.

I was born in 1954, and Nell was already almost twenty, but she lived on until I went to college, keeping an ample garden with my dad until the last couple of years. Even then I would see them sometimes leaning against each other down by the barn like old companions, heads close and shoulders touching.

Sometime during my second semester I got a phone call from my dad, which I knew meant something serious had happened. He said: "The mule died, son. I don't know what to do. Come home."

The Wonder of Small Things

My wife wakes me at 4AM.
Dreaming of tragedy, I gather
all my attention, sit up to listen.
"There's a little creature
sleeping in my yellow towel!"

she whispers, as if we might wake it
thirty feet below and on her studio
porch, the place she owns almost
entirely in a world that sometimes
lurches, seldom meets its promises,

sometimes kills. I pull on shorts and
follow. We have this right with each
other, to share discovery wherever
it startles us. I remember the night
she sang a small cotillion of southern

toads right to our feet, a February we
followed mating pairs of purple
salamanders up and down our swollen
creek, a season we watched the yellow
Argiope above our transom as she courted

with her mate, folding a thousand eggs
into a silken sheet which she hung behind her
before she desiccated. So much more,
a daily wonder. A grace. We walk the narrow
porch to see what it might hold, enfold, this:

one tiny, speckled wren, feathers puffed
against the first cold night, hanging
inside a fold of cloth which she gathers
around her, head under wing, inside a
temporary necessary shelter, breathing.

Subjects Suitable for Poetry

Those buttercups that ran along the walkway
of your grandmother's house, and the red begonias
she dug out of the ground every September
to bring into the warm kitchen, a woodstove,
a little table with flowers on it.

I could say this, hepatica in spring,
green fire upon a common grackle's wing,
the first snow, a first kiss, the last wish,
fresh cherries in a China dish,
a hundred tree frogs singing in a swamp.

Everywhere we look the earth displays
a tenderness of purpose.
What can we do but open our voices?

Acknowledgements

"As the Land Changes. . .," "Leonora," "Class Will Out," and "Gurley and Nell" have all been published or are forthcoming from *Braided Way,* a platform family I'm proud to be part of.

"Weather Bound" was published in the 2022 edition of *Pine Mountain Sand and Gravel.*

"Ruby and Darling," "Nearly Winter," "Field Peas," and "Figs" were awarded prizes or mentions by the North Carolina Poetry Society and published in *Pinesong Magazine.*

"Coyote" was published in the 2022 edition of *Kakalak Journal.*

"The Wonder of Small Things" was published in 2023 in *Indelible.*

"My Grandmother" also appeared in my first book, *The Boy the Brave Girls.*

I am deeply indebted to Liora Mondlak and her poetry group, who dragged me out of the pandemic and inspired me to write again, to the amazing Black Socks Poets who school and inspire me, to Charlotte Lit and the community of poets I met with for over a year and who made this collection possible. Vivian Bikulege and Linda Vigen Phillips were ideal readers, honest, perceptive and supportive.

The great poet Debra Kaufman helped with the final edit and Micaelah Scott Peterson of The Farthest Pixel did the cover illustration. Amanda Robertson, you're a dream to work with.

My closest deepest richest most generous poetry mentors were Dannye Romine Powell and Lola Haskins. I love them both and consider them part of my earth family.

I bow to my grandmothers, to the loving family that raised me, to my luminous sons and their families, to my many teachers, to the living earth.

And to my wife Ilana Dubester, collaborator, tender lover, found family, final editor.

Feel free to write me: *garfield@boxturtleroad.com.*

About the Author

Gary Phillips is the former poet laureate of Carrboro, North Carolina. He lives in a rammed earth house with his wife Ilana Dubester. A child of Appalachia, Gary reads poetry and Afro-Futurism, studies amphibian activities on full moon nights and remembers his grandmothers. His book of poetry and occasional pieces, *The Boy the Brave Girls,* was printed in 2016 by Human Error Publishing (Wendell, Mass). Write him at garfield@boxturtleroad.com.